THE BASICS OF WEIGHT TRAINING RECORD

Jim Bennett

Allyn and Bacon
Boston · London · Toronto · Sydney · Tokyo · Singapore

Series Editor: Suzy Spivey
Editorial Assistant: Jennifer Strada
Production Editor: Catherine Hetmansky
Cover Designer: Suzanne Harbison
Manufacturing Buyer: Megan Cochran

ISBN 0-205-17371-3

Printed in the United States of America

10 9 8 7 6 5 4 3 2 1   99 98 97 96 95 94

CONTENTS

How To Use
The Basics of Weight Training Record

Weight Training Objectives

A successful weight training program requires a well planned objective and purpose. Whether your training objective is to tone muscle and reduce your percentage of body fat, gain weight and build muscle, or just establish and maintain a high level of physical fitness, it is important to have your short- and long-term training objectives clearly laid out. This will keep you focused on your ultimate fitness goal and help you in determining where you are in the process of achieving your training objectives.

It is important before your first workout to consult with your physician concerning your training objectives. If your physician is unfamiliar with weight training, ask to have a stress test performed. If your training objectives are realistic and attainable and your health is good, your physician will give you the go-ahead that will increase your incentive to start your weight training without hesitation.

To take advantage of the many life-long health benefits associated with general fitness and competitive bodybuilding, you must make a strong commitment to the activity. Knowledge is a key factor in becoming successful in achieving your training objectives. In some instances, persons new to weight training are unfamiliar with the activity and expect significant changes in a short period of time. When establishing your training objectives, it is important to understand that your health, weight, and body measurements cannot change in a short period of time. The daily changes will be too small to observe, but after six to eight weeks you should be able to see changes beginning to take place in your appearance.

Measurement Record

Your beginning measurements should be taken on the day you begin your weight training program, before you start your first exercise. After your beginning measurements are recorded always have your measurements taken again at one-month intervals.

1

Next, determine the measurement goals you would like to achieve at the end of the first month. Under the column "1st Mo./Goal" enter your goals. At the end of the first month have your measurements taken again and compare them with your goals. Re-establish a new set of goals for the next month and work toward achieving them.

The term "RHR" represents your resting heart rate. To determine your resting heart rate it must be taken during a period of minimum stress. This can be accomplished by taking your pulse first thing in the morning before you get out of bed. Your resting heart rate, in comparison with your target heart rate (70%) for most bodybuilders (220 minus your age, then multiplied by 0.7), will give you an indication of your cardiovascular health. For example, if you are 35 years old, subtract 35 from 220 which equals 185. Then multiply 185 by 0.7. Your answer is a target heart rate of 130.

The term "% Fat" represents your percentage of body fat. This can be determined mathematically using your body measurements, mechanically using a caliper which pinches the skin, hydrostatically using water or electronically using a small electric current passing through your body. Each method is used to determine the ratio of body fat to body mass.

Daily Weight Training Record
Realizing progress or re-establishing training objectives can only be accomplished by maintaining an accurate record of each workout. By recording your exercises, sets, reps, weights, and workout comments you will be able to look back over a period of time to determine the amount and rate of progress. This will add to your enthusiasm and determination to achieve the training objectives you have set out to accomplish.

Along the top of the training record are spaces for recording the date, time of day, and your body weight. The lines below "Exercise" is where you will record the names of the various exercises performed, followed by the number of repetitions executed and weight used for up to six sets. Along the bottom of the page is space to record notes regarding the circumstances affecting your workout, and daily calorie, protein, carbohydrate, and fat intake. It is to your benefit to record daily nutritional intake, mood, length and quality of the previous night's sleep, and any other factors that may affect the quality of your workout.

Gaining Weight
And Building Muscle

Gaining weight and building muscle is very simple. Begin a progressive resistance exercise program combined with a proper diet. These are the only two building blocks that will allow you to achieve your desired results. Using progressively heavier weights and varying the training intensity will promote increased muscle size and strength as your body begins to adapt to the new demands. You must also modify your diet and eating schedule to to accommodate up to six smaller meals throughout the day. Each meal should include foods which contain a greater amount of protein and carbohydrate calories. This will fuel muscle recovery and growth.

Your muscles are made of protein, therefore, you need more than just protein to achieve gains in strength and size. To satisfy your basic metabolic requirements you must eat foods to replace the carbohydrates, fat, and protein used each day. This is accomplished by proportionately increasing your non-protein calories and protein consumption. This will provide the additional protein your body will require for muscle recovery and growth.

When daily protein and carbohydrate consumption is less than what is required to adequately fuel your weight training, your progress will slow down or virtually stop. If this is the case, your body will begin using muscle (protein) for energy. When training to increase muscle strength and size, and an <u>increased</u> amount of protein and carbohydrate calories are proportionately available in your diet, you will begin to make greater achievements.

Fueling Your
Weight Training Program

To properly fuel your weight training program, it is important to be aware of the number of calories your body requires each day. [1]The National Research Council has established Recommended Dietary Allowances (RDA) for people involved in a moderate to active level of activity. The number of calories required each day by activity level is as follows:

Level of Activity

Moderate — General fitness bodybuilding, walking 4 mph
Active — Competitive bodybuilding (high intensity)

Daily Calorie Requirements For Men and Women

Activity Level	Men	Women
Moderate	21 Calories/lb body weight	18 calories/lb body weight
Active	26 calories/lb body weight	22 calories/lb body weight

Use the following example to determine your daily calorie requirements at your present weight based on your level of activity:

A moderately active man with general fitness training objectives weighs 150 pounds. To determine his maximum daily calorie requirements, he multiplies his body weight by 21, which equals 3,150. This figure represents the total number of calories his metabolism requires <u>each day</u> to maintain itself and adequately fuel his weight training activity.

Using the chart on the next page, determine your ideal weight by your sex, height and frame size. When you have determined your ideal body weight, use the same formula, (i.e. ideal body weight of 160 pounds, multiplied by 21, equals 3,360 calories per day). In our example, to reach an ideal body weight of 160 lbs., would require 3,360 calories each day or <u>210 additional</u> calories beyond

MEN				WOMEN				
Height Feet Inches	Small Frame	Medium Frame	Large Frame	Height Feet Inches		Small Frame	Medium Frame	Large Frame
5 2	128-134	131-141	138-150	4	10	102-111	109-121	118-131
5 3	130-136	133-143	140-153	4	1	1103-113	111-123	120-134
5 4	132-138	135-145	142-156	5	0	104-115	113-126	122-137
5 5	134-140	137-148	144-160	5	1	106-118	115-129	125-140
5 6	136-142	139-151	146-164	5	2	108-121	118-132	128-143
5 7	138-145	142-154	149-168	5	3	111-124	121-135	131-147
5 8	140-148	145-157	152-172	5	4	114-127	124-138	134-151
5 9	142-151	148-160	155-176	5	5	117-130	127-141	137-155
5 10	144-154	151-163	158-180	5	6	120-133	130-144	140-159
5 11	146-157	154-166	161-184	5	7	123-136	133-147	143-163
6 0	149-160	157-170	164-188	5	8	126-139	136-150	146-167
6 1	152-164	160-174	168-192	5	9	129-142	139-153	149-170
6 2	155-168	164-178	172-197	5	10	132-145	142-156	152-173
6 3	158-172	167-182	176-202	5	1	1135-148	145-159	155-176
6 4	162-176	171-187	181-207	6	0	135-148	145-159	155-176

Build study, Society of Actuaries and Association of Life Insurance Medical Directors of America.

what is required to remain at a present body weight of 150. To reach an ideal weight of 140, he would have to consume <u>210 fewer</u> calories than what is required to remain at his present body weight.

Basic Nutritional Information

1. One calorie contains the energy required to raise the temperature of one Kilogram of water one degree Centigrade.

2. One pound of body fat contains approximately 3,500 calories.

3. Fat provides the body with energy required between meals and during prolonged exercise.

4. The three basic food sources required by the body are carbohydrate, protein and fat. Carbohydrates and fat are used by the body for energy. Protein is used for building tissue and body maintenance.

5. Fat contains 9 calories per gram; protein contains 4 calories per gram; and carbohydrates contain 4 calories per gram.

6. When you consume more calories than your body requires, the extra calories will be stored as fat for future use.

7. A diet must be nutritious, balanced and include an adequate amount of the basic nutrients: protein, carbohydrates, fat, vitamins, minerals, and water.

Protein Intake

Protein is used to build, repair, and maintain muscle, ligaments and tendons. It is not a primary energy source. When involved in weight training, muscle tissue is broken down and a process called anabolism rebuilds the muscle. Protein is what drives the anabolism process. When the amount of protein in your diet increases, your body will build new muscle tissue. If protein intake is insufficient, protein (muscle) will be broken down and used for energy. To determine the amount of protein in your present diet conduct a nutritional inventory of your food intake during the past 24 hours and record the results in the following table:

Meal	Total Calories	Protein Grams	Carbohydrate Grams	Fat Grams
Breakfast				
Lunch				
Dinner				
Snacks				
Total				

[2]The recommended amount of daily protein consumption for persons involved in weight training is 1.76 grams per kilogram of body weight. Unfortunately, the body has a limit to the amount of protein it can use for building muscle. Excess protein may be converted to fat. At a weight of 160 pounds (73kg), you would require a minimum of 128 grams of protein each day. No net gains or losses are realized with a protein consumption of 1.41 grams per kilogram of body weight. Therefore, any increase in dietary protein consumption above 1.41 g/kgbw will allow the body to form more proteins, a process stimulated by weight training. Use the chart on the following page to determine your specific protein needs.

This doesn't mean the more protein you eat above and beyond 1.76 g/kgbw, the greater gains you will achieve in muscle strength

Suggested Daily Protein Consumption					
Body Weight	KG/Body Weight	Protein	Body Weight	KG/Body Weight	Protein
100	45	80 gm	200	91	160 gm
110	50	88 gm	205	93	164 gm
115	52	92 gm	210	95	168 gm
120	54	96 gm	215	98	172 gm
125	57	100 gm	220	100	176 gm
130	59	104 gm	225	102	180 gm
135	61	108 gm	230	104	184 gm
140	64	112 gm	235	107	188 gm
145	66	116 gm	240	109	192 gm
150	68	120 gm	245	111	196 gm
155	70	124 gm	250	113	200 gm
160	73	128 gm	255	116	204 gm
165	75	132 gm	260	118	208 gm
170	77	136 gm	265	120	212 gm
175	79	140 gm	270	122	216 gm
180	82	144 gm	275	125	220 gm
185	84	148 gm	280	127	224 gm
190	86	152 gm	285	129	228 gm
195	88	156 gm	290	132	232 gm

Grams are rounded up to the nearest whole number.

and size. [2] A protein intake of 2.4 g/kgbw will not provide any additional benefits. Typical sources of protein are egg whites, skinless chicken (white meat), skinless turkey (white meat), and fish. Don't limit your meals to breakfast, lunch, and dinner alone. Your metabolism can only assimilate up to 30 grams of protein at each meal. The rest is stored for energy. Try to structure your schedule to eat 5-6 small meals throughout the day. In addition to the typical sources of protein there are many excellent high protein foods and supplements available to help increase your protein intake without increasing fat intake.

Carbohydrate Intake

Carbohydrates are the least abundant nutrient stored in the body and the main source of fuel for energy. Nutritionists recommend that your diet contain 60 to 65 percent carbohydrates when involved in intense physical activity. This recommendation equals a daily carbohydrate intake of about 3 to 4 grams per pound of body weight.

During digestion, complex carbohydrates are broken down into glucose. Glucose travels through the circulatory system as the main source of energy for refueling liver and muscle glycogen burned during exercise. Simple sugars are divided into two categories. Monosaccharides such as the glucose and fructose in fruit, and disaccharides such as lactose, or milk sugar which is made up of glucose and galactose. In some instances, simple sugars can cause a relatively sharp increase in blood sugar which can cause increased insulin release resulting in increased fat storage.

Starchy carbohydrates are made up of polysaccharides and provide a slower, more steady release of glucose into the bloodstream. Glucose from starchy carbohydrates causes minimum insulin secretion and provides greater sustained energy levels. A popular source of starchy carbohydrates is oatmeal, grits, potatoes, sweet potatoes, brown rice, yams, lima beans, kidney beans, peas, lentils, and other legumes. Fibrous plants and salad vegetables such as asparagus, broccoli, cauliflower, carrots, celery, green beans, and zucchini slow the release of carbohydrates into the bloodstream even more.

Fat Intake

To use fat as an effective source of energy, sufficient carbohydrate must be present in your diet. Understanding the various types of fat will help you in achieving the reduction in body fat required to meet your specific training objectives.

Essential fatty acids (EFAs) are important in numerous biological functions, including prostaglandins, which are necessary to help regulate almost every system in your body. EFAs are essential to properly fuel your body for weight training. They are used in several muscle building processes such as increasing glutamine levels, releasing growth hormone, and keeping connective tissue and cell membranes strong and healthy.

If you are maintaining a low-fat diet, a supplement may be necessary to provide an adequate supply of EFAs. A popular source of EFAs is sunflower, safflower, linseed, or flaxseed oil. Foods containing body fat such as beef are referred to as long-chain triglycerides (LCTs). LCTs must first be broken down in the intestines before they can be digested. Enzymes reduce the fat into fatty acids which travel across the membrane of the intestines where they are converted back into fat. At this point, they are transported by the lymphatic system to the neck and released into the circulatory system. This is the type of fat you want to avoid.

The American Heart Association advises that the percentage of fat calories in the American diet should be 30% or less. To achieve a reduction in body fat, people involved in weight training should limit their fat calorie intake to 20–25 percent. Use the following formula to calculate the percentage of fat calories in a food item:

1. Check the nutritional information for total calories and grams of fat per serving.

2. Multiply the number of fat grams by 9. This will give you the number of calories from fat.

3. Divide the number of calories from fat by the number of calories in a serving. The answer will be less than 1.

4. Multiply this number by 100 to get the percentage of calories from fat. If a serving of swiss cheese has 110 calories and 8 grams of fat, multiply 8 by 9 to get 72. Then divide 72 by 110 to get .65 and multiply by 100. The cheese you are eating yields 65% of its calories from fat.

[1]National Academy of Sciences, *Recommended Dietary Allowances*. 1980, 9th edition.

[2]Tarnopolsky M.A., Atkinson S.A., MacDougal J.D. et al. Evaluation of protein requirements of trained strength athletes. *Journal of Applied Physiology*. 1992;73:1986-95.

Losing Body Fat

Losing weight and inches is very simple. Become involved in a regular cardiovascular exercise program and develop an understanding of the foods you frequently eat. These are the only two building blocks that can produce a lean, healthy, functional, and vibrant body. Fad diets, diet pills, or fasting will not provide the lasting results you can achieve from understanding your eating habits and becoming involved in a regular cardiovascular exercise program.

Weight training (anaerobic) alone will not improve your cardiovascular (aerobic) endurance. Rather weight training, combined with cardiovascular training such as running, cycling, swimming, skipping rope or stepping will significantly improve your <u>overall</u> cardiovascular health. Cardiovascular training is defined as an activity that stimulates heart and lung activity producing beneficial changes in the body.

The flow of blood to the muscles increases when performing weight training exercises. For this reason, progressive cardiovascular training will help reduce body fat, increase oxygen and nutrient uptake, improve stress tolerance, and lower your blood pressure. The duration of the exercise can be from 20-30 minutes for high impact and up to 45-60 minutes for low impact aerobics.

By performing an aerobic activity that will stimulate a 70 percent target heart rate, over time you will begin to achieve a significant reduction in body fat. In most instances, people involved in aerobics are not aware of this fact. A reduction in body fat can be only be accomplished by working the cardiovascular system to its full potential. Your 70 percent target heart rate is equal to 220 minus your age, then multiplied by 0.7. Increasing your aerobic activity level to a 70 percent target heart rate will stimulate the reduction in body fat you have been striving to reach. Since your metabolic rate slows down in the evening, to help your metabolism maximize food utilization and minimize fat storage, try to eat your last meal before 8:00 p.m.

The Eight Basic Principles Of Weight Training

Weight training is individualized and can only be designed according to your particular anatomy, physiological condition and goals. Since no two people have the same body type, height or weight, they stand little chance of attaining the same results if they train identically. So how do you determine which is the best weight training program for you? The answer lies in understanding and applying the eight basic principles of weight training and evaluating their effects. These basic principles apply to everyone, but how each principle is applied will depend on you.

1. Overload — This principle is defined as increasing the resistance to movement or frequency and duration of activity. To promote increased muscle growth, strength and endurance you must go above and beyond what your muscles have become accustomed to. Without overloading your muscles, it will be impossible to achieve any significant gains. The four methods used to overload muscles are:

1. Increasing the resistance.
2. Increasing the number of repetitions.
3. Increasing the rate of work.
4. Increasing the amount of work in the same time period.

Each method is different and should be included in your training program with the percentages of each varying according to your training objectives. In general, increasing the resistance will promote increased muscle size and strength; increasing the number of repetitions performed will promote improved muscle endurance; increasing the rate of work will give you more power; and increasing the amount of work performed will allow you greater gains in your overall strength and endurance. Too much of an increase can result in overtraining.

2. Universality — This is defined as the all-around development principle. You must develop muscle strength and endurance together with all the major muscles, joints and support structures. Universality will serve as a base for high intensity, specialized training and development which is essential for competitive bodybuilding and other sports.

3. Gradualness — The demands placed on your muscles must progress gradually in both volume and intensity. Physical ability and immediate level of fitness will determine your rate of increase. No matter how hard you try, you will not realize significant improvement in a short period of time. The only method known to achieve long-lasting results is to adhere to gradualness. This can not be over-emphasized. If you reach a plateau in your weight training, do not become alarmed. It may be an indication that you need to vary one or more of these eight weight training principles.

4. Progressiveness — This principle is closely related to gradualness and overload. When stimulating muscle to adapt to greater workloads, over a period of time there must be an increase in the amount of weight used. This weight increase will be greater when beginning weight training and become less when muscles become more developed.

5. Repetition — Performing repetitions with light to moderate weight is the only way to learn how to properly perform an exercise and provoke certain physiological changes to take place in your body. When learning how to correctly perform an exercise, performing repetitions will allow you to develop the proper technique. If you begin using heavy weights, you will not learn the correct technique. When your technique is faulty, you will not be working the muscle properly. This can lead to possible injury.

6. Consistency — If you are to realize any change in your muscle size, strength and body measurements you must commit yourself to a regular weight training schedule. The minimum being two days a week. Your body will respond only when exercises are performed on a regular basis. This is where you come face-to-face with your commitment to achieve your specific health and fitness goals. Achieving maximum results will require a strong commitment to your workouts and training objectives.

7. Individualism — Your health, age, sex, and level of fitness will determine how well you can perform certain exercises. If you are in your mid-teens, elderly, or in poor physical health, using light weights and performing 8-12 repetitions is advisable. This will allow you to slowly adapt to your weight training program without subjecting yourself to possible injury.

8. Awareness — To successfully achieve your weight training goals and objectives, it is necessary to develop an understanding of the basic principles of weight training. With this as the foundation of your weight training program, it will generate the enthusiasm and desire to make weight training a consistent part of your lifestyle. Knowledge builds muscle and fitness!

Muscle Strength
And Endurance

To achieve the full benefits from weight training, it is necessary to develop and maintain a well-rounded training program that exercises all the major muscle groups. Muscle strength and endurance can only be developed by the overload principle. This is accomplished by increasing the amount of weight used or increasing the frequency and duration of sets and reps performed. Muscular strength is best developed by using heavier weights and performing 6-8 repetitions. Muscle endurance is developed by using lighter weight and performing 10-25 repetitions. To some extent, muscular strength and endurance are developed using each method, but each favors a more specific development. The intensity of your weight training can be changed by varying the amount of weight used, repetitions performed, number of sets, and rest interval. To gain improvement in both muscular strength and endurance, most experts recommend 8-12 repetitions per set.

Any degree of overload will result in strength development, but performing repetitions at or near the maximum weight that can be used for only one rep will provide the greatest achievements in strength. Your expected gains are limited to your initial level of strength and potential for improvement. To achieve the greatest gains, keep your routine rhythmical, performed at a moderate to slow speed, and for maximum benefit always perform the exercise through its full range of motion.

The combination of frequency, intensity, and duration of exercise is the most effective method for producing successful results. The interaction of these variables provide the overload stimulus required for increased muscle strength and endurance.

A Weight Training Partner

The best way to maintain a strong commitment to your training objectives is with a training partner. You are less likely to miss a workout if you are obligated to meet another person at the gym at a specific time. As you train together, you will develop a competitive edge and drive each other to perform at a greater intensity. Performing more reps or using a greater amount of weight during the next set in an effort to beat your last best is a very satisfying and rewarding accomplishment.

During your first workouts you will meet old friends or make new acquaintances with the same training objectives. Since most people would like a training partner–be selective. You will want to train with someone who can provide additional enthusiasm to get the most out of your workouts.

Weight Training Safety

The introduction of weight training safety is often a neglected topic in gyms and fitness centers. When one individual fails to follow proper safety procedures, he or she, along with other people nearby, become candidates for injury. For this reason, it is important to become familiar with and incorporate the following safety rules into your weight training:

 • **Inspect equipment for wear and tear.** Before beginning an exercise walk around the equipment to look for worn or loose fittings, frayed cables, and dry unlubricated guide rods.

 • **Use a spotter when performing demanding exercises.** Always use a spotter when using extra heavy weights. If you are unsure of your ability, ask another person to spot you.

 • **Weight training alone.** When weight training at home or at a gym with few people around, make another person aware of your activities and ask them to check on you periodically.

 • **Barbell catch racks.** A barbell catch rack is used to hold the barbell before performing exercises such as the bench press or squat. When used properly, a catch rack will allow you to safely perform the exercise and prevent an errant barbell from causing injury to yourself and others.

• **Barbell collars.** Barbell collars are metal clamps placed on the ends of a barbell to prevent the weight plates from sliding off when performing an exercise. If your fitness center or gym does not have collars available, insist that they get some.

• **Wear a weight lifting belt.** Weight lifting belts come in a wide variety of widths, thicknesses, and material. When used properly it will protect your abdominals and back from possible injury when performing movements with heavy weights, such as the squat, and deadlift.

> **Important:** Wearing a tightly cinched weight lifting belt when resting or performing exercises that do not directly involve the back or abdominals can significantly raise your blood pressure.

• **Never hold your breath.** Holding your breath beyond what is required for the initial movement will limit the flow of oxygen to your brain. If held too long, it could cause you to black out. You could be seriously injured if you experience dizziness or blackout during your set.

It makes no difference how you breathe as long as you breathe during the exercise. When you are unsure, the best thing to do is to breathe normally. This will keep you from blacking out or experiencing a feeling of dizziness. If you must follow a breathing pattern, the one most often used is inhaling during least resistance and exhaling during maximum resistance.

• **Return equipment when finished.** When you finish performing an exercise always return weight plates, dumbbells, barbells, and miscellaneous equipment to their appropriate location. Leaving them on the floor or propped up against a wall will only be setting yourself or another person up for possible injury. When the equipment is returned to its proper place, you will not have to search the gym or fitness center for that one missing item. This is just common courtesy.

• **Train with a certified instructor.** If your fitness center or gym advertises that they have trained, certified instructors on staff, by all means make good use of them. New members often weight train without supervision and watch other people performing exercises that are unfamiliar. They then attempt to perform the same exercise themselves. This is referred to as "Monkey See – Monkey Do." The new gym member could sustain possible injury because they may not understand the exercise and specific precautions. An instructor can prevent the development of poor form and bad habits.

• **Always warm-up before and cool-down after weight training.** Beginning your weight training without a proper warm-up can subject you to possible injury. A proper warm-up will increase your pulse rate, overall body temperature, blood and oxygen flow to specific muscles, and mentally prepare you for your weight training session. If you are limited by time, a few laps around the running track or a few minutes on a stationary bike or stepping machine is better than performing no warm-up at all.

The two types of warm-up programs are general and specific. The general warm-up includes large muscle activities such as aerobics, jogging, skipping rope, stationary cycling and stretching, and should last 10-15 minutes. The specific warm-up will prepare the muscle group to be exercised by performing 1-2 light, but progressively heavier sets prior to weight training with heavy weights.

The cool-down should immediately follow your weight training and should last 5-15 minutes. This will allow your body to recover from your weight training session and begin to cool down. The cool-down should include the same activities as the general warm-up, but performed at a more casual pace, like easy power walking, jogging, stepping, and stationary cycling.

Length Of Rest
Interval Between Sets

The rest interval between sets will depend upon your present level of fitness. During an average weight training session you should rest up to one minute between sets. This will give your body time to recover from the previous set and prepare for the next one. The rest interval will be shorter when working smaller muscle groups such as biceps and triceps and longer when working larger muscle groups such as legs and back. If you begin to feel light-headed after a set, take an extended rest interval to regain your composure. Try reducing the number of reps or amount of weight used in the next set.

Exercising
With Proper Form

The manner in which you perform an exercise is important if you are to achieve maximum results from your workouts. Performing an exercise correctly places the greatest load on the muscle group being worked. Sacrificing form for additional weight will always yield poor results. Bringing other body parts into the movement, such as jerking, or swinging a weight or body part to get moving is called cheating.

When performing an exercise, it is important to maintain the recommended body position and move the body joint/muscle through its full range of motion. The muscle being worked should be allowed to move from full extension to full contraction and back to full extension during each repetition. Movements shorter than this will not allow the muscle to work up to its full capacity.

Split Routines

During the first month of weight training you will workout a minimum of two non-consecutive days a week. This will give your muscles 48 hours between workouts to recover. A popular method to increase the weight training intensity is to split your routine to work two or more muscle groups on a different day. This is known as a split routine. In the basic split routine you will work three muscle groups on Monday and Thursday, and remaining muscle groups on Tuesday and Friday. The following is an example of a four-day split routine. Abs and calves are worked on alternate days.

4-Day Routine

Monday - Thursday	Tuesday - Friday
Abs	Abs
Chest	Legs
Triceps	Biceps/Forearms
Shoulders	Back
Calves	Calves

To intensify your weight training even further, you can choose either a five- or six-day split routine. The five-day split routine divides your weight training so you are exercising the same muscle groups on alternate days. The following is an example of a five-day split routine. Every other Monday routine is alternated with Tuesday.

5-Day Routine

Monday - Wednesday - Friday	Tuesday - Thursday
Abs	Abs
Legs	Chest
Biceps/Forearms	Triceps
Back	Shoulders
Calves	Calves

The six-day split routine is the most intense workout program you can follow. This is normally the training schedule followed by men and women who are involved in advanced competitive bodybuilding. The following is an example of a six-day split routine.

6-Day Routine

Mon - Thurs	Tues - Fri	Wed - Sat
Abs	Abs	Abs
Chest	Triceps	Legs
Shoulders	Biceps	Back
Calves	Forearms	Calves

Recovering From Your Workout

Your muscles grow in size and strength when you are *not* weight training. To take it a step further, the recovery process is at work not only when you are not weight training, but when you are completely at rest. If you have provided your metabolism with an adequate supply of protein and carbohydrates, anabolism will reach its peak when you are experiencing high-quality sleep. Once asleep, the growth hormone testosterone continues to increase since late afternoon to its peak in the early morning. The growth hormone cortisol, an anti-inflammatory catabolic hormone follows an opposite pattern.

The recovery process will take from 48-72 hours depending on the intensity of your weight training. This process itself will require you to rest periodically during the day and achieve high-quality sleep in the evening. Periodic resting consists of taking a 15 to 30 minute rest period, evenly spaced during the day. This may become a necessity when the intensity of your weight training has increased or when you find yourself becoming overstressed.

A rest period involves lying down or reclining on a soft surface and letting go both physically and mentally. This will normally refresh and recharge your energy level. Sleep requirements vary considerably between individuals. The norm for most people is eight hours of sleep a night. Some individuals function at 100% with only four or five hours per night and others require ten to twelve hours before they consider beginning their day. Let your body dictate how much sleep you need. This will allow you to rise alert, energetic, and ready to start the day.

Advanced Weight Training

You may reach a level in your weight training when you want to make greater gains in muscle size and strength. There are several techniques which can be incorporated into your weight training to help you achieve significant gains.

After warming-up the specific muscle group to be exercised, the remaining sets will be taken to the point of failure. This is when you can no longer complete a rep without additional help. There are two methods used to bring your muscles to the point of failure; forced reps, and strip sets. Other techniques such as compound sets, trisets, negative reps, and forced negatives will also increase the intensity of your weight training.

Forced Reps — Forced reps are performed with a training partner or spotter. After your muscle is taken to the point of failure, your training partner will apply minimum pressure to help you complete your rep. An example would be the bench press. Your training partner stands at the head of the bench and lightly pulls up on the bar with enough pressure to keep it moving. Each additional rep would require your training partner to apply more pressure.

Strip Sets — This is a method by which weight is progressively removed from an exercise machine or barbell during the execution of an exercise. Using the bench press as an example, place two spotters at opposite ends of the bar to remove a predetermined amount of weight each time you reach the point of failure. The bar should be plate loaded with a variety of plates so you can perform 4-6 repetitions with strict form. After reaching the point of failure without resting, have spotters remove a predetermined amount of weight from each end of the bar. Perform another set until you reach the point of failure and again, remove more weight. If you are still going strong, repeat the process again to the point of total muscle fatigue. When finished, you will experience a "pumped" sensation you have never felt before.

Compound Sets — Compound sets increase the intensity of your weight training by performing two exercises back to back with no rest interval between sets, followed by a normal rest interval.

Trisets — Trisets are identical to compound sets except that three exercises are performed, one after the other, followed by a normal rest interval. Trisets can be performed with any muscle group or combination of muscle groups.

Negative Reps — Negative reps are performed by lowering the weight at a much slower pace than it was raised.

Forced Negatives — Forced negatives are performed with exercise machines and free weights. After the weight is raised, you will resist additional negative pressure being applied by your training partner or spotter. When performing pure negatives, you will be able to use a weight 30-50% heavier. Your training partner will provide the necessary assistance to raise the weight to the starting position.

Overtraining

There are two types of overtraining, general and local. General overtraining affects the whole body producing stagnation and decreased physical performance. When local overtraining occurs, only one specific body part or muscle group is affected. Local overtraining can be experienced by most persons involved in weight training and is recognized by soreness and stiffness after performing a particular exercise.

When overtraining is not acknowledged and allowed to become serious, it can take weeks or even months for your body to recover. Overtraining must not be confused with exhaustion. Exhaustion is a reaction to the short-term imbalance between stress and how your body is adapting to it. Overtraining is the result of a prolonged imbalance with many obvious characteristics. It is important to understand and recognize the warning signs of overtraining and take the necessary steps to alleviate the problem before it gets worse.

The following characteristics can be used to identify an approaching "overtrained" condition:

1. You experience a noticeable decrease in your strength or performance level.

2. Overall fatigue. You don't recover from previous workouts as well as you did before. You become susceptible to headaches, colds, and fever blisters.

3. General muscle soreness. You experience a slow, general increase in muscle soreness and stiffness after a workout.

4. You sleep longer than normal and still feel tired.

5. You begin to realize a drop in body weight. This is an easy sign to spot when no effort is being made to lose weight.

6. Your resting heart rate is higher than normal. To check your resting heart rate, take your pulse everyday under the same conditions. If your resting heart rate is 10 beats higher than normal, your metabolism has not yet recovered from the previous workout. It normally takes 90 minutes to 2 hours for your pulse to return to normal, even after a short workout.

7. Your coordination becomes impaired. It has become difficult to perform exercises with the same pace and coordination you had in previous workouts.

8. Your body temperature is higher than normal. You begin to feel hot and feverish. This is an important sign that you may be reaching the point of heat exhaustion or heat stroke.

9. You begin to lose your appetite. This could be one of the reasons for a decrease in body weight.

10. The recovery time between sets and workouts is longer than normal.

11. You experience a swelling of the lymph nodes in your neck, groin, or armpits. This, along with an increased body temperature, is a symptom requiring immediate attention.

12. You become psychologically and emotionally drained. This includes increased nervousness, depression, inability to relax and poor motivation.

Your body has a limited capacity to adapt in a short period of time and when it is overstressed, you will begin to experience the symptoms of overtraining.

Saunas and Steambaths

A great place to relax after a hard workout is in either a steambath or sauna. Sauna heat and steam will have varying effects on your body and skin. Therefore, it is necessary to understand their differences for safe use.

The air in a sauna is heated by hot, porous rocks that radiate a constant, long-lasting heat. A sauna is similar to a convection oven in that the heat is evenly distributed over your body. If you take a higher seat in a sauna the air will be significantly hotter. The steambath is different from a sauna in that water vapor in the air radiates the heat. A steambath may seem considerably hotter than a sauna but it is actually several degrees cooler; 120°F for the steambath versus 170° to 180°F for the sauna. This is because body heat is more efficiently dissipated in dry air.

When the outside air temperature rises above 98.6°F, the blood vessels in the skin begin to dilate, allowing more blood to pass through them. The heat from your blood is then transferred to the surface of the skin. As your body temperature rises, signals are transmitted from temperature sensors in your lower brain to the sweat glands in your skin. This is when you begin to sweat. The fluid that is produced is 99.1% water and is drawn from the blood to the surface of the skin. With sweat on your skin, the excess body heat can be used to evaporate the water. Thus, sweating lets your body rid itself of excess heat.

Within hours of using a sauna or steambath, people have experienced an improved sense of well-being, increased energy and reduced muscle soreness. To be most effective, use the sauna or steambath 2-3 or more hours after weight training.

If you are pregnant, prolonged exposure to heat should be avoided. Check with your obstetrician if you intend to use a sauna or steambath. The same caution applies when using a whirlpool.

Weight Training Exercises

The following is a list according to muscle group worked of the exercises found in <u>The Basics of Weight Training Workbook</u>. If you have any questions regarding the proper execution and correct form when performing a particular exercise, refer to your workbook or consult with a certified instructor.

Abdominal Exercises

Bent-Knee Hanging Leg Raise
Crunches
Flat Bench Leg Raise
Incline Sit-Up
Reverse Sit-Up
Reverse Trunk Twist
Rope Pull-Down
Seated Knee-Up
Sit-Up
Support Vert. Leg Raise
Twisting Crunches

Chest Exercises

Adjust-A-Bar Dip
Bench Press
Bent-Arm Pullover
Bent-Over Cable Crossover
Decline Bench Press
Dumbbell Flye
Dumbbell Pull-Over
Incline Bench Press
Incline Dumbbell Flye

Tricep Exercises

45-degree Lying Tricep Ext.
Behind-The-Back Dips
Dumbbell Kickbacks
Lying Cross Face Tricep Ext.
Lying Tricep Extension
One-Arm Tricep Extension
Reverse-Grip Pushdown
Seated Tricep Extension
Tricep Pushdowns

Bicep Exercises

Alternate Dumbbell Curl
Concentration Curl
Hammer Curl
Incline Biceps Curl
Preacher Curl
Pulley Curl
Reverse Bicep Curl

Forearm Exercises

Barbell Wrist Curl
One-Arm Dumbbell Wrist Curl
Radial Flexion
Reverse Wrist Curl
Ulnar Flexion

Back Exercises

Back Raise
Bent-Over Barbell Row
Bent-Over Dumbbell Row
Lat Pulldown
Narrow Grip Lat Pulldown

Seated Pulley Rowing
Shoulder Shrug
T-Bar Bent-Over Row
Wide-Grip Chin-Up

Shoulder Exercises

Behind The Neck Press
Bent-Over Cable Lateral
Dumbbell Press
Front Arm Raise
Incline Lateral Arm Raise

Overhead Press
Prone Lateral Raise
Side Lateral Raise
Upright Row

Leg Exercises

Deadlift
Front Squat
Good Morning
Hack Squat
Leg (Hip) Abduction
Leg Adduction

Leg Curl
Leg Extension
Leg Press
Lunge
Squat

Calf Exercises

Calf Raises
Donkey Calf Raises

Seated Calf Raises
Standing Calf Raises

Short-Term
Training Objectives

consistency

Long-Term
Training Objectives

Angel Basset arms.

Measurement Record

	Beginning	1st Month	Goal	2nd Month	Goal	3rd Month	Goal	4th Month	Goal	5th Month	Goal
Date											
Neck											
Shoulders											
Chest											
Upper Arm											
Forearm											
Waist											
Oblique											
Hips											
Upper Thigh											
Lower Thigh											
Calf											
Weight											
Height											
RHR											
% Fat											

Measurement Record

	6th Month	Goal	7th Month	Goal	8th Month	Goal	9th Month	Goal	10th Month	Goal	11th Month	Goal
Date												
Neck												
Shoulders												
Chest												
Upper Arm												
Forearm												
Waist												
Oblique												
Hips												
Upper Thigh												
Lower Thigh												
Calf												
Weight												
Height												
RHR												
% Fat												

29

Date _____ **Weight** _____ **Time** _____

Exercise	1		2		3		4		5		6	
	Rep	Wt	Rep	Wt	Rep	Wt	Rep	Wt	Rep	Wt	Rep	Wt

Notes: _____

Total Calorie Intake: _____ Protein Intake: _____ Carb. Intake: _____ Fat Intake: _____

Date _____ **Weight** _____ **Time** _____

Exercise	1		2		3		4		5		6	
	Rep	Wt	Rep	Wt	Rep	Wt	Rep	Wt	Rep	Wt	Rep	Wt

Notes:

Total Calorie Intake: _____   Protein Intake: _____   Carb. Intake: _____   Fat Intake: _____

Date _____ **Weight** _____ **Time** _____

Exercise	1 Rep	Wt	2 Rep	Wt	3 Rep	Wt	4 Rep	Wt	5 Rep	Wt	6 Rep	Wt

Notes:

Total Calorie Intake: _____ Protein Intake: _____ Carb. Intake: _____ Fat Intake: _____

Date _____ **Weight** _____ **Time** _____

Exercise	1	Rep	Wt	2	Rep	Wt	3	Rep	Wt	4	Rep	Wt	5	Rep	Wt	6	Rep	Wt

Notes: _____

Total Calorie Intake: _____   Protein Intake: _____   Carb. Intake: _____   Fat Intake: _____

Date _____ **Weight** _____ **Time** _____

Exercise	1		2		3		4		5		6	
	Rep	Wt	Rep	Wt	Rep	Wt	Rep	Wt	Rep	Wt	Rep	Wt

Notes: _____

Total Calorie Intake: _____   Protein Intake: _____   Carb. Intake: _____   Fat Intake: _____

Date _____ **Weight** _____ **Time** _____

Exercise	1 Rep	Wt	2 Rep	Wt	3 Rep	Wt	4 Rep	Wt	5 Rep	Wt	6 Rep	Wt

Notes: _____

Total Calorie Intake: _____   Protein Intake: _____   Carb. Intake: _____   Fat Intake: _____

Date _____ **Weight** _____ **Time** _____

Exercise	1	Rep	Wt	2	Rep	Wt	3	Rep	Wt	4	Rep	Wt	5	Rep	Wt	6	Rep	Wt

Notes: _____

Total Calorie Intake: _____ **Protein Intake:** _____ **Carb. Intake:** _____ **Fat Intake:** _____

Exercise

Date _____ **Weight** _____ **Time** _____

	1		2		3		4		5		6	
	Rep	Wt	Rep	Wt	Rep	Wt	Rep	Wt	Rep	Wt	Rep	Wt

Notes: _____

Total Calorie Intake: _____ Protein Intake: _____ Carb. Intake: _____ Fat Intake: _____

Date _____ **Weight** _____ **Time** _____

Exercise	1		2		3		4		5		6	
	Rep	Wt	Rep	Wt	Rep	Wt	Rep	Wt	Rep	Wt	Rep	Wt

Notes:

Total Calorie Intake: _____ Protein Intake: _____ Carb. Intake: _____ Fat Intake: _____

Date _____ **Weight** _____ **Time** _____

Exercise	1		2		3		4		5		6	
	Rep	Wt	Rep	Wt	Rep	Wt	Rep	Wt	Rep	Wt	Rep	Wt

Notes: _____

Total Calorie Intake: _____ Protein Intake: _____ Carb. Intake: _____ Fat Intake: _____

Date _____ Weight _____ Time _____

Exercise	1		2		3		4		5		6	
	Rep	Wt	Rep	Wt	Rep	Wt	Rep	Wt	Rep	Wt	Rep	Wt

Notes:

Total Calorie Intake: _____   Protein Intake: _____   Carb. Intake: _____   Fat Intake: _____

Date _____ **Weight** _____ **Time** _____

Exercise	1 Rep	Wt	2 Rep	Wt	3 Rep	Wt	4 Rep	Wt	5 Rep	Wt	6 Rep	Wt

Notes:

Total Calorie Intake: _____ Protein Intake: _____ Carb. Intake: _____ Fat Intake: _____

Date _____ **Weight** _____ **Time** _____

Exercise	1		2		3		4		5		6	
	Rep	Wt	Rep	Wt	Rep	Wt	Rep	Wt	Rep	Wt	Rep	Wt

Notes:

Total Calorie Intake: _____ Protein Intake: _____ Carb. Intake: _____ Fat Intake: _____

Date _____ **Weight** _____ **Time** _____

Exercise

	1		2		3		4		5		6	
	Rep	Wt	Rep	Wt	Rep	Wt	Rep	Wt	Rep	Wt	Rep	Wt

Notes: _____

Total Calorie Intake: _____   Protein Intake: _____   Carb. Intake: _____   Fat Intake: _____

Date _____ **Weight** _____ **Time** _____

Exercise	1	Rep	Wt	2	Rep	Wt	3	Rep	Wt	4	Rep	Wt	5	Rep	Wt	6	Rep	Wt

Notes:

Total Calorie Intake: _____ **Protein Intake:** _____ **Carb. Intake:** _____ **Fat Intake:** _____

Date _____ **Weight** _____ **Time** _____

Exercise	1		2		3		4		5		6	
	Rep	Wt	Rep	Wt	Rep	Wt	Rep	Wt	Rep	Wt	Rep	Wt

Notes:

Total Calorie Intake: _____   Protein Intake: _____   Carb. Intake: _____   Fat Intake: _____

Date _____ **Weight** _____ **Time** _____

Exercise

	1		2		3		4		5		6	
	Rep	Wt	Rep	Wt	Rep	Wt	Rep	Wt	Rep	Wt	Rep	Wt

Notes: _____

Total Calorie Intake: _____ **Protein Intake:** _____ **Carb. Intake:** _____ **Fat Intake:** _____

Date _____ **Weight** _____ **Time** _____

Exercise	1		2		3		4		5		6	
	Rep	Wt	Rep	Wt	Rep	Wt	Rep	Wt	Rep	Wt	Rep	Wt

Notes:

Total Calorie Intake: _____ **Protein Intake:** _____ **Carb. Intake:** _____ **Fat Intake:** _____

Date _____ Weight _____ Time _____

Exercise	1 Rep	Wt	2 Rep	Wt	3 Rep	Wt	4 Rep	Wt	5 Rep	Wt	6 Rep	Wt

Notes:

Total Calorie Intake: _____ Protein Intake: _____ Carb. Intake: _____ Fat Intake: _____

Date _____ **Weight** _____ **Time** _____

Exercise	1 Rep	Wt	2 Rep	Wt	3 Rep	Wt	4 Rep	Wt	5 Rep	Wt	6 Rep	Wt

Notes: _____

Total Calorie Intake: _____   Protein Intake: _____   Carb. Intake: _____   Fat Intake: _____

Date _____ **Weight** _____ **Time** _____

Exercise	1		2		3		4		5		6	
	Rep	Wt	Rep	Wt	Rep	Wt	Rep	Wt	Rep	Wt	Rep	Wt

Notes:

Total Calorie Intake: _____ Protein Intake: _____ Carb. Intake: _____ Fat Intake: _____

Exercise   Date _____   Weight _____   Time _____

Exercise	1		2		3		4		5		6	
	Rep	Wt	Rep	Wt	Rep	Wt	Rep	Wt	Rep	Wt	Rep	Wt

Notes: _____

Total Calorie Intake: _____   Protein Intake: _____   Carb. Intake: _____   Fat Intake: _____

Date _____ **Weight** _____ **Time** _____

Exercise	1 Rep	Wt	2 Rep	Wt	3 Rep	Wt	4 Rep	Wt	5 Rep	Wt	6 Rep	Wt

Notes: _____

Total Calorie Intake: _____ Protein Intake: _____ Carb. Intake: _____ Fat Intake: _____

Date _____ Weight _____ Time _____

Exercise	1	Rep	Wt	2	Rep	Wt	3	Rep	Wt	4	Rep	Wt	5	Rep	Wt	6	Rep	Wt

Notes:

Total Calorie Intake: _____ Protein Intake: _____ Carb. Intake: _____ Fat Intake: _____

Date _____ **Weight** _____ **Time** _____

Exercise	1		2		3		4		5		6	
	Rep	Wt	Rep	Wt	Rep	Wt	Rep	Wt	Rep	Wt	Rep	Wt

Notes: _____

Total Calorie Intake: _____ Protein Intake: _____ Carb. Intake: _____ Fat Intake: _____

Date _____ **Weight** _____ **Time** _____

Exercise	1		2		3		4		5		6	
	Rep	Wt	Rep	Wt	Rep	Wt	Rep	Wt	Rep	Wt	Rep	Wt

Notes:

Total Calorie Intake: _____ Protein Intake: _____ Carb. Intake: _____ Fat Intake: _____

Date _____ **Weight** _____ **Time** _____

Exercise

	1	Wt	2	Wt	3	Wt	4	Wt	5	Wt	6	Wt
	Rep		Rep		Rep		Rep		Rep		Rep	

Notes: _____

Total Calorie Intake: _____ Protein Intake: _____ Carb. Intake: _____ Fat Intake: _____

Date _____ **Weight** _____ **Time** _____

Exercise	1 Rep	Wt	2 Rep	Wt	3 Rep	Wt	4 Rep	Wt	5 Rep	Wt	6 Rep	Wt

Notes:

Total Calorie Intake: _____   Protein Intake: _____   Carb. Intake: _____   Fat Intake: _____

Date _____ **Weight** _____ **Time** _____

Exercise	1		2		3		4		5		6	
	Rep	Wt	Rep	Wt	Rep	Wt	Rep	Wt	Rep	Wt	Rep	Wt

Notes: _____

Total Calorie Intake: _____ Protein Intake: _____ Carb. Intake: _____ Fat Intake: _____

Date _____ **Weight** _____ **Time** _____

Exercise	1	Wt	2	Wt	3	Wt	4	Wt	5	Wt	6	Wt
	Rep		Rep		Rep		Rep		Rep		Rep	

Notes:

Total Calorie Intake:　　　Protein Intake:　　　Carb. Intake:　　　Fat Intake:

Date _____ Weight _____ Time _____

Exercise	1 Rep	Wt	2 Rep	Wt	3 Rep	Wt	4 Rep	Wt	5 Rep	Wt	6 Rep	Wt

Notes:

Total Calorie Intake: _____   Protein Intake: _____   Carb. Intake: _____   Fat Intake: _____

Date _____ **Weight** _____ **Time** _____

Exercise	1		2		3		4		5		6	
	Rep	Wt	Rep	Wt	Rep	Wt	Rep	Wt	Rep	Wt	Rep	Wt

Notes:

Total Calorie Intake: _____   Protein Intake: _____   Carb. Intake: _____   Fat Intake: _____

Exercise   **Date** _____   **Weight** _____   **Time** _____

Exercise	1	Rep	Wt	2	Rep	Wt	3	Rep	Wt	4	Rep	Wt	5	Rep	Wt	6	Rep	Wt

Notes:

Total Calorie Intake: _____   Protein Intake: _____   Carb. Intake: _____   Fat Intake: _____

Exercise | **Date** _____ **Weight** _____ **Time** _____

Exercise	1	Rep	Wt	2	Rep	Wt	3	Rep	Wt	4	Rep	Wt	5	Rep	Wt	6	Rep	Wt

Notes:

Total Calorie Intake: _____ Protein Intake: _____ Carb. Intake: _____ Fat Intake: _____

Date _____ **Weight** _____ **Time** _____

Exercise	1		2		3		4		5		6	
	Rep	Wt	Rep	Wt	Rep	Wt	Rep	Wt	Rep	Wt	Rep	Wt

Notes: _____

Total Calorie Intake: _____ Protein Intake: _____ Carb. Intake: _____ Fat Intake: _____

Date _____ **Weight** _____ **Time** _____

Exercise	1		2		3		4		5		6	
	Rep	Wt	Rep	Wt	Rep	Wt	Rep	Wt	Rep	Wt	Rep	Wt

Notes: _____

Total Calorie Intake: _____   Protein Intake: _____   Carb. Intake: _____   Fat Intake: _____

Date _____ **Weight** _____ **Time** _____

Exercise

	1		2		3		4		5		6	
	Rep	Wt	Rep	Wt	Rep	Wt	Rep	Wt	Rep	Wt	Rep	Wt

Notes: _____

Total Calorie Intake: _____ Protein Intake: _____ Carb. Intake: _____ Fat Intake: _____

Date _____ **Weight** _____ **Time** _____

Exercise	1		2		3		4		5		6	
	Rep	Wt	Rep	Wt	Rep	Wt	Rep	Wt	Rep	Wt	Rep	Wt

Notes: _____

Total Calorie Intake: _____ Protein Intake: _____ Carb. Intake: _____ Fat Intake: _____

Exercise | **Date** _____ | **Weight** _____ | **Time** _____

Exercise	1	Rep	Wt	2	Rep	Wt	3	Rep	Wt	4	Rep	Wt	5	Rep	Wt	6	Rep	Wt

Notes: _____

Total Calorie Intake: _____   Protein Intake: _____   Carb. Intake: _____   Fat Intake: _____

Date ___ **Weight** ___ **Time** ___

Exercise

	1		2		3		4		5		6	
	Rep	Wt	Rep	Wt	Rep	Wt	Rep	Wt	Rep	Wt	Rep	Wt

Notes: _____

Total Calorie Intake: _____ Protein Intake: _____ Carb. Intake: _____ Fat Intake: _____

Date _____ **Weight** _____ **Time** _____

Exercise	1		2		3		4		5		6	
	Rep	Wt	Rep	Wt	Rep	Wt	Rep	Wt	Rep	Wt	Rep	Wt

Notes:

Total Calorie Intake: _____   Protein Intake: _____   Carb. Intake: _____   Fat Intake: _____

Date _____ Weight _____ Time _____

Exercise	1		2		3		4		5		6	
	Rep	Wt	Rep	Wt	Rep	Wt	Rep	Wt	Rep	Wt	Rep	Wt

Notes:

Total Calorie Intake: Protein Intake: Carb. Intake: Fat Intake:

Exercise **Date** _____ **Weight** _____ **Time** _____

Exercise	1	Rep	Wt	2	Rep	Wt	3	Rep	Wt	4	Rep	Wt	5	Rep	Wt	6	Rep	Wt

Notes:

Total Calorie Intake: _____   Protein Intake: _____   Carb. Intake: _____   Fat Intake: _____

Date _____ **Weight** _____ **Time** _____

Exercise	1		2		3		4		5		6	
	Rep	Wt	Rep	Wt	Rep	Wt	Rep	Wt	Rep	Wt	Rep	Wt

Notes: _____

Total Calorie Intake: _____ Protein Intake: _____ Carb. Intake: _____ Fat Intake: _____

Date _____ Weight _____ Time _____

Exercise	1		2		3		4		5		6	
	Rep	Wt	Rep	Wt	Rep	Wt	Rep	Wt	Rep	Wt	Rep	Wt

Notes:

Total Calorie Intake: _____ Protein Intake: _____ Carb. Intake: _____ Fat Intake: _____

Date _____ **Weight** _____ **Time** _____

Exercise	1		2		3		4		5		6	
	Rep	Wt	Rep	Wt	Rep	Wt	Rep	Wt	Rep	Wt	Rep	Wt

Notes:

Total Calorie Intake: _____ **Protein Intake:** _____ **Carb. Intake:** _____ **Fat Intake:** _____

Date _____ Weight _____ Time _____

Exercise

Exercise	1		2		3		4		5		6	
	Rep	Wt	Rep	Wt	Rep	Wt	Rep	Wt	Rep	Wt	Rep	Wt

Notes: _____

Total Calorie Intake: _____ Protein Intake: _____ Carb. Intake: _____ Fat Intake: _____

Date _____ **Weight** _____ **Time** _____

Exercise

Exercise	1		2		3		4		5		6	
	Rep	Wt	Rep	Wt	Rep	Wt	Rep	Wt	Rep	Wt	Rep	Wt

Notes:

Total Calorie Intake: _____ Protein Intake: _____ Carb. Intake: _____ Fat Intake: _____

Date _____ **Weight** _____ **Time** _____

Exercise	1		2		3		4		5		6	
	Rep	Wt	Rep	Wt	Rep	Wt	Rep	Wt	Rep	Wt	Rep	Wt

Notes:

Total Calorie Intake: _____ Protein Intake: _____ Carb. Intake: _____ Fat Intake: _____

Date _____ **Weight** _____ **Time** _____

Exercise	1 Rep	Wt	2 Rep	Wt	3 Rep	Wt	4 Rep	Wt	5 Rep	Wt	6 Rep	Wt

Notes: _____

Total Calorie Intake: _____ Protein Intake: _____ Carb. Intake: _____ Fat Intake: _____

Exercise | **Date** _____ | **Weight** _____ | **Time** _____

Exercise	1	Rep	Wt	2	Rep	Wt	3	Rep	Wt	4	Rep	Wt	5	Rep	Wt	6	Rep	Wt

Notes:

Total Calorie Intake: _____   Protein Intake: _____   Carb. Intake: _____   Fat Intake: _____

Exercise | **Date** _____ **Weight** _____ **Time** _____

Exercise	1	Wt	2	Wt	3	Wt	4	Wt	5	Wt	6	Wt
	Rep		Rep		Rep		Rep		Rep		Rep	

Notes: _____

Total Calorie Intake: _____ Protein Intake: _____ Carb. Intake: _____ Fat Intake: _____

Date _____ **Weight** _____ **Time** _____

Exercise	1	Rep	Wt	2	Rep	Wt	3	Rep	Wt	4	Rep	Wt	5	Rep	Wt	6	Rep	Wt

Notes:

Total Calorie Intake: _____   Protein Intake: _____   Carb. Intake: _____   Fat Intake: _____

Date _____ **Weight** _____ **Time** _____

Exercise	1 Rep	Wt	2 Rep	Wt	3 Rep	Wt	4 Rep	Wt	5 Rep	Wt	6 Rep	Wt

Notes: _____

Total Calorie Intake: _____ Protein Intake: _____ Carb. Intake: _____ Fat Intake: _____

Date _____ **Weight** _____ **Time** _____

Exercise	1 Rep	Wt	2 Rep	Wt	3 Rep	Wt	4 Rep	Wt	5 Rep	Wt	6 Rep	Wt

Notes:

Total Calorie Intake: _____ Protein Intake: _____ Carb. Intake: _____ Fat Intake: _____

Date _____ **Weight** _____ **Time** _____

Exercise	1	Wt	2	Rep	Wt	3	Rep	Wt	4	Rep	Wt	5	Rep	Wt	6	Rep	Wt
	Rep		Rep														

Notes:

Total Calorie Intake: _____ Protein Intake: _____ Carb. Intake: _____ Fat Intake: _____

Date _____ **Weight** _____ **Time** _____

Exercise	1		2		3		4		5		6	
	Rep	Wt	Rep	Wt	Rep	Wt	Rep	Wt	Rep	Wt	Rep	Wt

Notes:

Total Calorie Intake: _____   Protein Intake: _____   Carb. Intake: _____   Fat Intake: _____

Date _____ **Weight** _____ **Time** _____

Exercise	1		2		3		4		5		6	
	Rep	Wt	Rep	Wt	Rep	Wt	Rep	Wt	Rep	Wt	Rep	Wt

Notes: _____

Total Calorie Intake: _____ Protein Intake: _____ Carb. Intake: _____ Fat Intake: _____

Date _____ **Weight** _____ **Time** _____

Exercise	1 Rep	Wt	2 Rep	Wt	3 Rep	Wt	4 Rep	Wt	5 Rep	Wt	6 Rep	Wt

Notes:

Total Calorie Intake: _____ Protein Intake: _____ Carb. Intake: _____ Fat Intake: _____

Date _____ **Weight** _____ **Time** _____

Exercise	1		2		3		4		5		6	
	Rep	Wt	Rep	Wt	Rep	Wt	Rep	Wt	Rep	Wt	Rep	Wt

Notes: _____

Total Calorie Intake: _____ Protein Intake: _____ Carb. Intake: _____ Fat Intake: _____

Exercise

Date _____ **Weight** _____ **Time** _____

Exercise	1	Rep	Wt	2	Rep	Wt	3	Rep	Wt	4	Rep	Wt	5	Rep	Wt	6	Rep	Wt

Notes: _____

Total Calorie Intake: _____   Protein Intake: _____   Carb. Intake: _____   Fat Intake: _____

Exercise | **Date** _____ **Weight** _____ **Time** _____

Exercise	1 Rep	Wt	2 Rep	Wt	3 Rep	Wt	4 Rep	Wt	5 Rep	Wt	6 Rep	Wt

Notes: _____

Total Calorie Intake: _____ Protein Intake: _____ Carb. Intake: _____ Fat Intake: _____

Date _____ **Weight** _____ **Time** _____

Exercise	1 Rep	Wt	2 Rep	Wt	3 Rep	Wt	4 Rep	Wt	5 Rep	Wt	6 Rep	Wt

Notes: _____

Total Calorie Intake: _____   Protein Intake: _____   Carb. Intake: _____   Fat Intake: _____

Date _____ **Weight** _____ **Time** _____

Exercise	1		2		3		4		5		6	
	Rep	Wt	Rep	Wt	Rep	Wt	Rep	Wt	Rep	Wt	Rep	Wt

Notes:

Total Calorie Intake: _____ Protein Intake: _____ Carb. Intake: _____ Fat Intake: _____

Date _____ **Weight** _____ **Time** _____

Exercise	1		2		3		4		5		6	
	Rep	Wt	Rep	Wt	Rep	Wt	Rep	Wt	Rep	Wt	Rep	Wt

Notes: _____

Total Calorie Intake: _____   Protein Intake: _____   Carb. Intake: _____   Fat Intake: _____

Date _____ **Weight** _____ **Time** _____

Exercise	1 Rep	Wt	2 Rep	Wt	3 Rep	Wt	4 Rep	Wt	5 Rep	Wt	6 Rep	Wt

Notes: _____

Total Calorie Intake: _____ Protein Intake: _____ Carb. Intake: _____ Fat Intake: _____

Date _____ **Weight** _____ **Time** _____

Exercise	1	Rep	Wt	2	Rep	Wt	3	Rep	Wt	4	Rep	Wt	5	Rep	Wt	6	Rep	Wt

Notes: _____

Total Calorie Intake: _____ Protein Intake: _____ Carb. Intake: _____ Fat Intake: _____

Date _____ **Weight** _____ **Time** _____

Exercise	1		2		3		4		5		6	
	Rep	Wt	Rep	Wt	Rep	Wt	Rep	Wt	Rep	Wt	Rep	Wt

Notes: _____

Total Calorie Intake: _____ Protein Intake: _____ Carb. Intake: _____ Fat Intake: _____

Exercise   **Date** _____   **Weight** _____   **Time** _____

Exercise	1 Rep	Wt	2 Rep	Wt	3 Rep	Wt	4 Rep	Wt	5 Rep	Wt	6 Rep	Wt

Notes:

Total Calorie Intake: _____   Protein Intake: _____   Carb. Intake: _____   Fat Intake: _____

Date _____ Weight _____ Time _____

Exercise	1 Rep	Wt	2 Rep	Wt	3 Rep	Wt	4 Rep	Wt	5 Rep	Wt	6 Rep	Wt

Notes:

Total Calorie Intake: _____ Protein Intake: _____ Carb. Intake: _____ Fat Intake: _____

Exercise | **Date** _____ | **Weight** _____ | **Time** _____

Exercise	1	Rep	Wt	2	Rep	Wt	3	Rep	Wt	4	Rep	Wt	5	Rep	Wt	6	Rep	Wt

Notes:

Total Calorie Intake: _____   Protein Intake: _____   Carb. Intake: _____   Fat Intake: _____

Date _____ **Weight** _____ **Time** _____

Exercise	1 Rep	Wt	2 Rep	Wt	3 Rep	Wt	4 Rep	Wt	5 Rep	Wt	6 Rep	Wt

Notes:

Total Calorie Intake: _____   Protein Intake: _____   Carb. Intake: _____   Fat Intake: _____

Date _____ Weight _____ Time _____

Exercise	1	Rep	Wt	2	Rep	Wt	3	Rep	Wt	4	Rep	Wt	5	Rep	Wt	6	Rep	Wt

Notes:

Total Calorie Intake: _____   Protein Intake: _____   Carb. Intake: _____   Fat Intake: _____

Date _____ **Weight** _____ **Time** _____

Exercise	1	Rep	Wt	2	Rep	Wt	3	Rep	Wt	4	Rep	Wt	5	Rep	Wt	6	Rep	Wt

Notes:

Total Calorie Intake: _____ Protein Intake: _____ Carb. Intake: _____ Fat Intake: _____

Date _____ Weight _____ Time _____

Exercise	1		2		3		4		5		6	
	Rep	Wt	Rep	Wt	Rep	Wt	Rep	Wt	Rep	Wt	Rep	Wt

Notes: _____

Total Calorie Intake: _____ Protein Intake: _____ Carb. Intake: _____ Fat Intake: _____

Date _____ Weight _____ Time _____

Exercise	1		2		3		4		5		6	
	Rep	Wt	Rep	Wt	Rep	Wt	Rep	Wt	Rep	Wt	Rep	Wt

Notes:

Total Calorie Intake: _____ Protein Intake: _____ Carb. Intake: _____ Fat Intake: _____

Date _____ **Weight** _____ **Time** _____

Exercise	1	Rep	Wt	2	Rep	Wt	3	Rep	Wt	4	Rep	Wt	5	Rep	Wt	6	Rep	Wt

Notes: _____

Total Calorie Intake: _____ Protein Intake: _____ Carb. Intake: _____ Fat Intake: _____

Date _____ **Weight** _____ **Time** _____

Exercise	1 Rep	Wt	2 Rep	Wt	3 Rep	Wt	4 Rep	Wt	5 Rep	Wt	6 Rep	Wt

Notes: _____

Total Calorie Intake: _____ Protein Intake: _____ Carb. Intake: _____ Fat Intake: _____

Date _____ **Weight** _____ **Time** _____

Exercise	1	Rep	Wt	2	Rep	Wt	3	Rep	Wt	4	Rep	Wt	5	Rep	Wt	6	Rep	Wt

Notes: _____

Total Calorie Intake: ____ Protein Intake: ____ Carb. Intake: ____ Fat Intake: ____

Date _____ Weight _____ Time _____

Exercise	1 Rep	Wt	2 Rep	Wt	3 Rep	Wt	4 Rep	Wt	5 Rep	Wt	6 Rep	Wt

Notes:

Total Calorie Intake: _____ Protein Intake: _____ Carb. Intake: _____ Fat Intake: _____

Date _____ **Weight** _____ **Time** _____

Exercise	1	Rep	Wt	2	Rep	Wt	3	Rep	Wt	4	Rep	Wt	5	Rep	Wt	6	Rep	Wt

Notes: _____

Total Calorie Intake: _____ Protein Intake: _____ Carb. Intake: _____ Fat Intake: _____

Date _____ **Weight** _____ **Time** _____

Exercise	1		2		3		4		5		6	
	Rep	Wt	Rep	Wt	Rep	Wt	Rep	Wt	Rep	Wt	Rep	Wt

Notes: _____

Total Calorie Intake: _____   Protein Intake: _____   Carb. Intake: _____   Fat Intake: _____

Date _____ **Weight** _____ **Time** _____

Exercise	1		2		3		4		5		6	
	Rep	Wt	Rep	Wt	Rep	Wt	Rep	Wt	Rep	Wt	Rep	Wt

Notes:
_____

Total Calorie Intake: _____   Protein Intake: _____   Carb. Intake: _____   Fat Intake: _____

Date _____ Weight _____ Time _____

Exercise	1		2		3		4		5		6	
	Rep	Wt	Rep	Wt	Rep	Wt	Rep	Wt	Rep	Wt	Rep	Wt

Notes: _____

Total Calorie Intake: _____   Protein Intake: _____   Carb. Intake: _____   Fat Intake: _____

Date _____ Weight _____ Time _____

Exercise	1	Rep	Wt	2	Rep	Wt	3	Rep	Wt	4	Rep	Wt	5	Rep	Wt	6	Rep	Wt

Notes: _____

Total Calorie Intake: _____   Protein Intake: _____   Carb. Intake: _____   Fat Intake: _____

Date _____ **Weight** _____ **Time** _____

Exercise	1		2		3		4		5		6	
	Rep	Wt	Rep	Wt	Rep	Wt	Rep	Wt	Rep	Wt	Rep	Wt

Notes: _____

Total Calorie Intake: _____ Protein Intake: _____ Carb. Intake: _____ Fat Intake: _____

Date _____ Weight _____ Time _____

Exercise	1	Rep	Wt	2	Rep	Wt	3	Rep	Wt	4	Rep	Wt	5	Rep	Wt	6	Rep	Wt

Notes:

Total Calorie Intake: _____ Protein Intake: _____ Carb. Intake: _____ Fat Intake: _____

Date _____ Weight _____ Time _____

Exercise	1		2		3		4		5		6	
	Rep	Wt	Rep	Wt	Rep	Wt	Rep	Wt	Rep	Wt	Rep	Wt

Notes: _____

Total Calorie Intake: _____   Protein Intake: _____   Carb. Intake: _____   Fat Intake: _____

Date _____ **Weight** _____ **Time** _____

Exercise	1		2		3		4		5		6	
	Rep	Wt	Rep	Wt	Rep	Wt	Rep	Wt	Rep	Wt	Rep	Wt

Notes: _____

Total Calorie Intake: _____ Protein Intake: _____ Carb. Intake: _____ Fat Intake: _____

Date _____ **Weight** _____ **Time** _____

Exercise	1		2		3		4		5		6	
	Rep	Wt	Rep	Wt	Rep	Wt	Rep	Wt	Rep	Wt	Rep	Wt

Notes:

Total Calorie Intake: _____ Protein Intake: _____ Carb. Intake: _____ Fat Intake: _____

Date _____ **Weight** _____ **Time** _____

Exercise	1	Wt	2	Rep	Wt	3	Rep	Wt	4	Rep	Wt	5	Rep	Wt	6	Rep	Wt
	Rep		Rep														

Notes: _____

Total Calorie Intake: _____ Protein Intake: _____ Carb. Intake: _____ Fat Intake: _____

Date _____ **Weight** _____ **Time** _____

Exercise	1		2		3		4		5		6	
	Rep	Wt	Rep	Wt	Rep	Wt	Rep	Wt	Rep	Wt	Rep	Wt

Notes: _____

Total Calorie Intake: _____ Protein Intake: _____ Carb. Intake: _____ Fat Intake: _____

Date _____ Weight _____ Time _____

Exercise	1		2		3		4		5		6	
	Rep	Wt	Rep	Wt	Rep	Wt	Rep	Wt	Rep	Wt	Rep	Wt

Notes:

Total Calorie Intake: _____   Protein Intake: _____   Carb. Intake: _____   Fat Intake: _____

Date _____ **Weight** _____ **Time** _____

Exercise	1		2		3		4		5		6	
	Rep	Wt	Rep	Wt	Rep	Wt	Rep	Wt	Rep	Wt	Rep	Wt

Notes:

Total Calorie Intake: _____ Protein Intake: _____ Carb. Intake: _____ Fat Intake: _____

Exercise

Date _____ **Weight** _____ **Time** _____

Exercise	1		2		3		4		5		6	
	Rep	Wt	Rep	Wt	Rep	Wt	Rep	Wt	Rep	Wt	Rep	Wt

Notes: _____

Total Calorie Intake: _____ Protein Intake: _____ Carb. Intake: _____ Fat Intake: _____

Date _____ **Weight** _____ **Time** _____

Exercise	1		2		3		4		5		6	
	Rep	Wt	Rep	Wt	Rep	Wt	Rep	Wt	Rep	Wt	Rep	Wt

Notes:

Total Calorie Intake: _____ Protein Intake: _____ Carb. Intake: _____ Fat Intake: _____

Date _____ Weight _____ Time _____

Exercise	1	Rep	Wt	2	Rep	Wt	3	Rep	Wt	4	Rep	Wt	5	Rep	Wt	6	Rep	Wt

Notes:

Total Calorie Intake: _____   Protein Intake: _____   Carb. Intake: _____   Fat Intake: _____

Exercise Log

Date _____ **Weight** _____ **Time** _____

Exercise	1		2		3		4		5		6	
	Rep	Wt	Rep	Wt	Rep	Wt	Rep	Wt	Rep	Wt	Rep	Wt

Notes: _____

Total Calorie Intake: _____ Protein Intake: _____ Carb. Intake: _____ Fat Intake: _____

Date _____ **Weight** _____ **Time** _____

Exercise	1		2		3		4		5		6	
	Rep	Wt	Rep	Wt	Rep	Wt	Rep	Wt	Rep	Wt	Rep	Wt

Notes:

Total Calorie Intake: _____   Protein Intake: _____   Carb. Intake: _____   Fat Intake: _____

Date _____ **Weight** _____ **Time** _____

Exercise	1		2		3		4		5		6	
	Rep	Wt	Rep	Wt	Rep	Wt	Rep	Wt	Rep	Wt	Rep	Wt

Notes:

Total Calorie Intake: _____ Protein Intake: _____ Carb. Intake: _____ Fat Intake: _____

Exercise **Date** _____ **Weight** _____ **Time** _____

	1		2		3		4		5		6	
	Rep	Wt	Rep	Wt	Rep	Wt	Rep	Wt	Rep	Wt	Rep	Wt

Notes:

Total Calorie Intake: _____ **Protein Intake:** _____ **Carb. Intake:** _____ **Fat Intake:** _____

Date _____ **Weight** _____ **Time** _____

Exercise

Exercise	1 Rep	Wt	2 Rep	Wt	3 Rep	Wt	4 Rep	Wt	5 Rep	Wt	6 Rep	Wt

Notes:

Total Calorie Intake: _____ Protein Intake: _____ Carb. Intake: _____ Fat Intake: _____

Date _____ **Weight** _____ **Time** _____

Exercise	1 Rep	Wt	2 Rep	Wt	3 Rep	Wt	4 Rep	Wt	5 Rep	Wt	6 Rep	Wt

Notes:

Total Calorie Intake: _____ **Protein Intake:** _____ **Carb. Intake:** _____ **Fat Intake:** _____

Date _____ **Weight** _____ **Time** _____

Exercise	1 Rep	Wt	2 Rep	Wt	3 Rep	Wt	4 Rep	Wt	5 Rep	Wt	6 Rep	Wt

Notes:

Total Calorie Intake: _____ Protein Intake: _____ Carb. Intake: _____ Fat Intake: _____

Date _____ **Weight** _____ **Time** _____

Exercise	1		2		3		4		5		6	
	Rep	Wt	Rep	Wt	Rep	Wt	Rep	Wt	Rep	Wt	Rep	Wt

Notes:

Total Calorie Intake: _____ Protein Intake: _____ Carb. Intake: _____ Fat Intake: _____